MARY FOR TODAY

HANS URS VON BALTHASAR

MARY FOR TODAY

Translated by
Robert Nowell and Abigail Tardiff

With illustrations by
Virginia Broderick

IGNATIUS PRESS   SAN FRANCISCO

Title of the German original:
Maria für heute
© 1997, 2016 Johannes Verlag Einsiedeln
Freiburg im Breisgau, Germany

The English translation of *Mary for Today*, except for the preface, was originally published by St. Paul Publications in 1987, based on the version printed by Verlag Herder in the same year. A preface by Hans Urs von Balthasar, taken from *L'Osservatore Romano* and included in the 2016 German edition by Johannes Verlag Einsiedeln, has been translated by Ignatius Press and added to this volume with permission.

Cover design by Roxanne Mei Lum

© 2022 Ignatius Press, San Francisco,
with permission of Johannes Verlag and St. Paul Publications
ISBN 978-1-62164-512-2 (PB)
ISBN 978-1-64229-193-3 (eBook)
Library of Congress Catalogue Number 2021953179
Printed in the United States of America ∞

CONTENTS

FOREWORD

By Edward Sri

Pope Saint John Paul II's 1987 encyclical *Redemptoris Mater* reminds us of Mary's *humanness*. Though the teaching in this magisterial text certainly deepens our understanding of the various Marian doctrines and invites us to greater reverence for and devotion to the Blessed Virgin Mary, it does so in a way that does not place Mary on so high a pedestal that she remains, as it were, out of reach—someone we might admire from afar but not someone to whom we could relate. John Paul II describes how Mary, though blessed with unique privileges and graces, remained one of us, a disciple who had to make an interior "pilgrimage of faith" (*Redemptoris Mater*, no. 15). Indeed, the words from Luke's Gospel "Blessed is she who believed" serve as an interpretive key to Mary. Like us, she had to abandon herself to the divine plan, even when things were not clear. Like us, she was called to heroic trust and self-emptying in times of suffering (nos. 15–18). Like us, she did not simply perform a one-time act of faith; she had to renew her fiat continually throughout her life. She herself experienced the joys and

7

trials of Christian discipleship, and she models for all Christians the way forward in their own walk with the Lord. As Hans Urs von Balthasar comments, *Redemptoris Mater* "places her near us, rather than raising her to inaccessible heights".[1]

Those words could describe this short work, *Mary for Today*, which Balthasar himself had published in 1987, the same year John Paul II's *Redemptoris Mater* was released. In his reflections on Marian doctrines and on Mary's journey as a disciple, Balthasar keeps the humanness of Our Lady in focus.

Take, for example, his explanation of the great mystery of the Virgin Birth. On one hand, Balthasar affirms the traditional Catholic understanding of Mary's remaining a virgin while giving birth ("in partu")—that Mary not only conceived Jesus as a virgin and remained a virgin throughout her life, but also remained a virgin in the act of delivering her child (and, as a result, did not experience pain when giving birth): "At the birth every pain was dissolved into pure light." He even underscores how, though the particulars of this miraculous event remain obscure, the Virgin Birth itself should not be difficult to accept: "How her womb opened and closed again we do not know, and it is pointless to speculate about an event that for God was child's play, something much less consequential than the original overshadowing by the Holy Spirit.

[1] Preface, p. 13.

Someone who accepts this first miracle as valid ...
should not lose any sleep over accepting the second
miracle, the Virgin Birth."[2]

On the other hand, Balthasar also explains that
the Virgin Birth does not mean Mary was superhuman and never experienced sufferings at all during
her pregnancy. No doubt, her husband's initial lack
of understanding about her pregnancy would have
been a suffering. The sudden move from Nazareth
to Bethlehem for the census would have been a suffering. Having to give birth to Jesus in conditions of
such poverty and humility would have been a suffering. And the burden of responsibility for carrying
a child—something every mother shoulders—was
something significantly weightier for Mary, for she
knew she carried in her womb not just any ordinary child, but the Messiah, the holy Son of God
(Lk 1:31–33, 35).

Mary certainly had her share of mental and spiritual pains along the way (and Balthasar even con-
templates the possibility of her experiencing various
physical discomforts until shortly before the miracle
of the Virgin Birth). Though she experienced the
most extraordinary of pregnancies, she still endured
various trials during those nine months, and those
trials remind us of how close she still remains to
the first mother, Eve; to all mothers throughout the
ages; and to all of Israel awaiting its Savior: "She

[2] Chapter 2, p. 37.

stands in solidarity with the mother of the race precisely because she is free of sin, and she stands even
more closely in solidarity with her people Israel,
which as a whole is continually experiencing the
birth pangs of the Messiah. She belongs to the completion of the covenant with the people that represents mankind as a whole."[3] While we know that
Mary conceived the Christ Child as a virgin by the
power of the Holy Spirit and that the Child passed
through her body miraculously in the Virgin Birth,
keeping in mind Mary's various kinds of sufferings
during those nine months helps us remember that
she still was human, still was a true mother—with
many of the joys and sufferings of a mother—and
still remains close to all of us as we journey through
this valley of tears.

Another example of the balance in understanding Mary's unique graces and her humanness can be
seen in Balthasar's reflections on the way she "kept
... and pondered" the mysteries of Christ in her
heart (Lk 2:19). Balthasar reminds us of how Mary's
Immaculate Conception—the fact that "from the
start she possesses the full grace of the Holy Spirit"—
gave her unique insight. Being "full of grace", Mary
possessed more understanding about her Son than
anyone else. So her "'pondering' over the facts she
has experienced and lived through cannot be a matter of just stumbling around in the dark".[4]

[3] Chapter 2, p. 35.
[4] Chapter 3, p. 49.

At the same time, Mary still needed to reflect on the mysterious events unfolding in her life and in the life of her Son. She continually mulled them over prayerfully, trying to understand their deeper meaning. The Bible reveals she had moments when she "did not understand" (Lk 2:50), moments when she had to consider "in her mind" what was being spoken to her (Lk 1:29) and moments when all she could do was keep and ponder these things in her heart (Lk 2:19). Von Balthasar rightly underscores that even with her unique revelations, graces, and privileges, Mary still had to grow in faith as a disciple: "By no means does she understand everything completely from the first moment onward; instead, she has to work tirelessly to understand all these overpowering ideas as well as she can."[5] She had unique wisdom, but it still had room to develop: her pondering points to what Balthasar calls "a quiet, silent growth in insight".[6]

Indeed, her own experience of conceiving a child as a virgin was such a profound mystery that no human being could fully understand. She was told she would conceive a child, not by man, but by the Holy Spirit. She was told that the child she would bear in her womb was "the Son of the Most High" (Lk 1:32). Balthasar asks, "How is a Jewish woman to grasp that Yahweh has a son? But her pregnancy is a fact. The Incarnation is a fact on which she is

---

[5] Chapter 3, p. 48.
[6] Chapter 3, p. 49.

continually to ponder without comprehending it."[7] Like us, Mary, though given singular graces and privileges, still needed to grow in her understanding of the mystery of her Son. She still had to walk by faith and not by sight.

In these and many other ways, Balthasar's *Mary for Today* reflects the spirit and wisdom of John Paul II's monumental Marian encyclical *Redemptoris Mater* and keeps Mary close to us. Or, to use Balthasar's own words again in application to this work, it places her near us, rather than raising her to inaccessible heights.

Feast of the Visitation, 2022

[7] Chapter 3, p. 48.

PREFACE

Mary in Our Time[*]

Pope John Paul II's encyclical on Mary, *Redemptoris Mater*, is a masterpiece because—even while Mary is so deserving of our reverence—it places her near us, rather than raising her to inaccessible heights. Throughout her whole life, she remained, like us, a believer. She believed the word the angel spoke to her, though the message seemed improbable. She believed even when she did not understand the words of her twelve-year-old son. She believed when she visited Jesus and he turned her away to start a new family, that of the believing Church. She believed when, from the Cross, he pointed her to a new son, who would introduce her into a Church of sinners. Today we often think that believing is more difficult now than it was for earlier generations, who were simply raised and culturally immersed in the Christian faith. But Mary had

[*] This essay by Hans Urs von Balthasar originally appeared (in Italian translation) as "Maria in nostro tempo" in *Il giornale del popolo*, June 13, 1987, p. 28. Translated from the German by Thomas Jacobi.

it just as hard as we do, if not harder. Therefore, as the pope explains, she is an example for the entire Church after her: she has already lived through all the difficulty of being a Christian, and in fact done this better than all others. This is why she is such a help to us, a model for the Church as a whole and for each individual. Just as humanity's inclination toward mutual help is one of its noblest and, at the same time, most natural qualities, so Mary as helper is the consummation of this virtue, a human virtue that anyone can understand.

Certainly, she is unique, the only one who brought the Savior bodily into the world. But are we not all called to give birth to Christ into our world so poor in faith—through our belief, our courage, our witness, our fruitfulness? Saints and spiritual writers have said this time and again. If there were no longer fruitful witnesses, this would show that Christianity was already extinguished. If it is to live on, determined men and women must invest themselves over and over in the continuation of the living faith. Nothing in Christianity works automatically. Giving birth ever anew to the "child" of Christianity requires following after the woman in her labors (the one who cries out in her birth pangs in Revelation 12). In this travail, the whole Church is Marian—men and women alike. Christ himself compares Christians to a woman who must give birth in pain before she can rejoice in the child who has just been brought into the world (Jn 16:21).

Paul goes to great lengths to explain that the Church, as a whole, is feminine with respect to Christ the Bridegroom (Eph 5). She is feminine as the Mother of Christ ("Man is now born of woman," 1 Cor 11:12), but also as his Bride, who must love him with reverence.

These statements bring us to some of the most important questions of today's culture. In our time, we struggle for equal dignity between man and woman, but often this means, in an all-too-masculine technical culture, that the woman strives to secure her place by conforming herself to specifically masculine functions. Yet such functions remain superficial and fruitless—and indeed, over time, prove destructive—if man no longer realizes that he himself sprang forth from the maternal, bridal fruitfulness of woman and owes himself to her. Many of the demands of feminism are understandable, but any attempt to smooth over the difference between the sexes into an ant-like neutrality, a sexlessness, would be a distortion.

The Catholic Church can be a luminous example to the broader culture. If Christ the God-man is her founder, then within her foundation there are two people of decisive importance: Mary and Peter. Mary, the perfectly sinless one, is the central form of the Church, insofar as this Church is "without blemish" (Eph 5:27). Peter, the chosen head of the Church's structural body [*des kirchlichen Organismus*] in the world, received his authority to lead from Christ, because of his faith (Mt 16:18) and despite his denial. In terms of worthiness, Mary stands high over Peter. She *is* the Church "without blemish"; Peter, as Christ's "representative", is only the "servant of the servants" (*servus servorum*), a sinner among sinful brothers and sisters. Thus it makes perfect sense that the more recent popes in particular—especially John Paul II—lift up their eyes to Mary, full of trust and awe.

This in particular, as I said above, could be a model to our culture, a culture that is constantly forgetting just what it owes to woman and to her distinctive femininity. Such feminine power cannot be grasped and graphed with the masculine science of statistics, but by no means is this a disadvantage. Rather, it is quite clearly an advantage, and a sign of its superiority. Although we obviously do not mean to equate the maternal, virginal ground of all human culture with the unique dignity and sanctity of Mary, the two nevertheless share one point in common: our whole overly masculine technical culture easily forgets how profoundly it owes its existence to the womanly source from which it springs. Men as individuals are ready to acknowledge how much they owe to woman, to mother or spouse; but our civilization, built up so predominantly by men, is hardly ready to do this—a proof of just how one-sided and thus how imperiled it is.

Modern feminism loves to push back against the creation account in Genesis, where woman is formed from man's rib and brought to him as a "helper". While such a reaction is understandable, it is quite superficial. For within this telling of the story lies another meaning: man without woman is helpless. Though he can name the animals, inventing labels for them, he finds nothing in them for himself, for his development, for his happiness. The woman given to him, the "helper", helps above all *to provide* meaning to his humanity. What use is his body's seed without a field in which to sow it? What use is his "constructive" intellect without a fertile spiritual soil where it can first develop in a meaningful way [*sinnvoll entfalten*]? Man's helplessness without woman is seen most clearly in the raising of a child, where the woman contributes incomparably more than the man. But one must not isolate the physiological realm from the spiritual and from the person as a whole: similar proportions can and should hold in every sphere of culture. Here, too—we repeat one last time—the Church must serve as a model: as indispensable as Peter's role is for the order of the Church, Mary is far more so, since without her there would be neither Christ nor his "Mystical Body" the Church, which is why Paul VI rightly referred to her as "Mother of the Church".

I

IN THE WILDERNESS

IN THE WILDERNESS

The Woman and the Dragon

The best way to learn something about Mary and her connection to our times is to start with chapter 12 of Revelation, for at the heart of this last book of the Bible are visionary images that provide insight into the drama of the world's history.

The "great portent ... in heaven", the "woman clothed with the sun, with the moon under her feet, and on her head a crown of twelve stars", but crying out in the pangs of birth, is without doubt first of all God's people, Israel, suffering the birth pangs of the Messiah. Israel is to give birth to something far more than an ordinary human being—but how can this come to pass? And the pains are not just internal: they are accompanied by a measureless fear of the monster, the fire-red dragon with his seven mouths open wide "that he might devour her child when she brought it forth".

But at Israel's prime, embodying its entire hope and its entire faith, a boy is born who, as a psalm says, "is to rule all the nations with a rod of iron"—a boy who, in other words, receives from God absolute power over creation: power even over death, power even over being swallowed up by the dragon, so that, rising again on the other side of death, he can be "caught up to God and to his throne". This culmination of Israel's faith was a particular human being called Mary, who bore the Messiah in the flesh and who experienced and suffered his entire fate with him up to his crucifixion and his ascent to the throne of God. What became of her?

It says first of all that she "fled into the wilderness, where she had a place prepared by God". But before we learn more about her, a decisive battle in heaven is portrayed: after the Messiah has been caught up into heaven, Michael and his angels fight against the dragon and his followers, who are not able to stand firm: "the great dragon, that ancient serpent, who is called the Devil and Satan, the deceiver of the whole world", is thrown down from the eternity of heaven to the finiteness of earth; heaven is full of rejoicing, but woe to the earth, "for the devil has come down to you in great wrath, because he knows that his time is short."

Now the dragon and the woman are once again opposed to each other; and the dragon has no other aim than to "pursue" the woman. We are now in the period after Christ, which in Revelation is always measured in the same way: "one thousand two hundred and sixty days" or "forty-two months" or, as here, "a time, and two times, and half a time". That means a time that seems twice as long to men and that yet (as it says elsewhere) has been "shortened (by half) for the sake of the elect".

This is precisely the age in which we live and also the age of the woman who was Israel, who became Mary, and who has finally become the mother of all Jesus' brothers and sisters today. In Revelation, Mary becomes the Church, since it is said that in his anger against the woman, the dragon "went off to make war on the rest of her offspring, on those who keep the commandments of God and bear testimony to Jesus."

The devil's rage against the Church is so great because it is not able to accomplish anything against her. "The woman was given the two wings of the great eagle that she might fly ... into the wilderness" to a place where, safe from the serpent, "she is to be nourished" throughout the history of the world. This security is a precarious security, since "the serpent poured water like a river out of his mouth after the woman, to sweep her away with the flood." But now "the earth came to the help of the woman, and the earth opened its mouth and swallowed the river which the dragon had poured from his mouth."

What a situation this is! The woman is fleeing, but her flight is successful, since she is given the wings of the great eagle: the wings of God, who, like the eagle, takes his young on his wings so that they may lose their fear and carries them out of the nest into the air. This was how Yahweh treated Israel. But to the little ones who are carried out into the empty spaces, this expanse must seem like nothing but wilderness. Nevertheless, it is precisely the wilderness that is the "place of safety" to which God brings the woman and where in a miraculous way he sees to her nourishment at this time of history, just as he had fed Israel in the desert. Back then, it was a geographical desert, one that today we could cross quickly in an airplane. But that is not possible with the wilderness where the Church must live—not before the end of time. Back then, there was an exodus toward a promised land. Today, no such land exists for the Church except that which is promised on the other side of history: a new heaven and a new earth.

The Church is an existence between what the dragon spews forth and the nourishment of heaven, threatened with death and yet protected in a place prepared by God; but at the same time, for all the Church's children, an existence in an incessant war against the satanic powers. The Church is not some entity to be differentiated from her children: she lives in them, as her children live through and in her. Hence their fate is hers: they are exposed to the rage of the serpent, and, if they fight, they are protected and nourished by God. "Your adversary the devil prowls around like a roaring lion, seeking someone to devour. Resist him, firm in your faith, knowing that the same experience of suffering is required of your brotherhood throughout the world" (1 Pet 5:8–9). "Put on the whole armor of God, that you may be able to stand against the wiles of the devil. For we are not contending against flesh and blood, but … against the world rulers of this present darkness" (Eph 6:11–12).

The powers are angry, not merely indifferent. After Christ, they developed into a trinity opposed to God, as Revelation describes them in detail: in the beast rising out of the sea, the old dragon created for himself a form dominating world history in which he was "worshipped" and to which the power was given "to make war on the saints and to conquer them". The Church can suffer defeats, be decimated and humiliated, until the final torment of which Christ spoke in the Gospels, until the encirclement of the "beloved city" mentioned in Revelation. "Now when these things begin to take place, look up and raise your heads, because your redemption is drawing near" (Lk 21:28).

In the history of the Church, it is not, therefore, a matter of a battle that will go her way on earth; for even when the children are fighting, she remains—as do her "offspring"—in the wilderness until the end of time. It is there, and only there, that, borne on the wings of God, she is protected. The wilderness is her promised land.

Spat upon and Nourished

Mary is "Mother Church" and at the same time "Mother of the Church." (She can be both, because at the foot of the Cross with the beloved disciple

she became the original image and very first cell
of the community founded by the Crucified One,
and at the same time she received the apostle, and
in him all Christians, as her children.) In the hidden seclusion of her earthly life, she experienced
beforehand everything that her children would later
encounter in the way of pain and consolation. What
someone like Paul loudly proclaimed about himself
as an example for everybody—that he was weak,
despised, homeless, indeed regarded as the world's
rubbish, and yet was never abandoned, never
despairing, never annihilated—is echoed in more
restrained tones in the life of Mary.

What must it have been like for her as her pregnancy, whose origins she did not disclose, became
clear to those around her—not just to Joseph, in
whose house she was not yet living, but to others
who, unlike her bridegroom, gave their tongues free
rein? And how did it improve matters when Joseph,
enlightened in a dream, took her as his wife? This
did not mean that the trouble that swirled around her
and around her child went away. Nor could Joseph
offer any kind of explanation that would calm things
down. People let it be and reconciled themselves to
the idea that this child must surely be Joseph's son.
In any case, when the time came for the mother's
purification, many thought that she certainly needed
this rite prescribed by "the law of Moses" (Lk 2:22).
We cannot say whether even later, perhaps until she
moved in with John, Mary did not have to deal with
people's suspicions.

But it is clear that after the commencement of Jesus' public activity, she must have lived in close contact with his relations, who, as John reports, did not believe in him but urged him to work miracles publicly, perhaps in order to make some money off of him (Jn 7:3–5). But when he went too far for them and people were coming to him from all over, "his friends ... went out to seize him, for they said, 'He is beside himself'" (Mk 3:21). Mary is in the midst of these people; she comes together with them to see him; Jesus is told that his mother and his brethren are standing outside; they send for him and call him, but he lets her wait outside the door and go home without having achieved her purpose (Mk 3:31–35). We must try to imagine what must have been going on inside this mother's mind: "Don't I count for anything with him anymore? Is he leaving me hanging?" She was hearing a mass of partially distorted rumors, and she surely was not receiving letters from him; she was living in a wilderness of concern and fear. How the Holy Spirit, who had once overshadowed her, nourished her in this wilderness we do not know. But perhaps it was above all with that which was most fruitful: a dark night of the senses and the soul that left her with the barest of faith, which finally enabled her to look on the horror of her child's crucifixion, at the same time losing him and being solemnly bequeathed to someone else as mother.

Of course she had known a mother's joys with her tiny, helpless baby as he slowly grew up: this has been portrayed to the point of tedium by hundreds of thousands of pictures of the Madonna. But who has painted for us the lonely woman spending endless days in anxiety and fear, who without a doubt did not understand what was really going on? She had heard of the sword that would pierce her own soul. But what form her suffering would take she could not know in advance. Upon that first catastrophe, when the twelve-year-old boy left his parents with no warning and then explained with gentle reproach that his place was in the temple, they did not understand. One cannot imagine that afterward, when they had returned to Nazareth, he gave them a full explanation to help dispel their confusion. It was enough that he "was obedient to them".

And certainly it is stated twice in the infancy narrative that Mary kept everything that was said about the child—and that he himself said—in her heart and pondered it in her mind. But the second mention comes just after the verse which says that "they did not understand the saying which he spoke to them." So she was considering what this incomprehensible thing could mean. She would not have done this if she did not know that the nature and fate of this young man were something unique and would be suitably revealed in the future. But just as Jesus had so little indication of the fate that lay in store for him but let it be revealed to him from day to day by his Father, so too would his mother have anticipated little of what was to come: part of her faith (the fulfillment of the faith of Abraham) was always to accept God's decrees. That is consistent with the poverty of spirit and purity of heart extolled in the beatitudes: today heart and mind are emptied out so that space may be created in them to behold God and his kingdom one day. It would be odd if Mary, once in heaven, were to disavow her earthly experience of faith and turn instead to giving Christians prophetic revelations about the future (the conversion of Russia and so on).

The abode assigned to the woman by God is the wilderness, and he himself bears her there on his eagle's wings. For the whole of world history, the Church must remember that she receives enough nourishment from God so as not to perish in the wilderness, and she is far enough from the serpent pursuing her that she will not be swept away by the flood it spews forth. That must suffice.

The Woman's Children Wage War

The woman's children are characterized by the fact that they "keep the commandments of God and bear testimony to Jesus". With John as with Paul, God's commandments are incorporated into the one commandment of love: to continue bearing witness with an attitude of patient, unshakeable perseverance despite all attacks and temptations. Here all that is necessary is "the endurance of the saints, those who keep the commandments of God and the faith of Jesus" (Rev 14:12).

Nowhere in the New Testament do Christians wage war with other weapons. Even the "whole armor of God" that Paul describes in detail (Eph 6:13–18) only specifies more clearly what Christians are to arm themselves with: truth, righteousness, readiness to proclaim the gospel, faith, confidence in salvation, the sword of the Spirit that is the word of God, continual prayer. These are purely "godly" and in no way earthly weapons. But Revelation, as the Gospels and various episodes of Paul's life had already made clear, indicates that these are the only effective weapons. "The weapons of our warfare are not worldly but have divine power to destroy strongholds. We destroy arguments and every proud obstacle to the knowledge of God" (2 Cor 10:4–5). We are to destroy fallacies, not overcome foreign countries and cultures and turn them Christian by force. This does not mean that Christians should just stay home: they have been commanded by the Lord to go out as missionaries into all the countries of the world. But they are to go with no weapons other than those used by their Lord and handed over to them: "Take nothing for your journey, no staff, nor bag, nor bread, nor money: and do not have two tunics" (Lk 9:3). When the Logos rides out to battle through the history of the world in his "robe dipped in blood" (Rev 19:11–16), followed by his "called and chosen and faithful" (Rev 17:14), it is with no other weapons than those that have been mentioned. The sharpest weapon is the two-edged sword that issues from the mouth of God's Word (Rev 1:16, 19:15), and that is nothing other than himself: he came into the world to bring "a sword" (Mt 10:34) that pierces as deeply as possible (Heb 4:12). Yes or no.

But it should be noted that, while the woman's children fight, the woman herself, though she is pursued, does not. The children can be overcome by the force of evil (Rev 11:7, 13:7); the woman, the Church as a virgin who gives birth, cannot. For the whole period of the history of the world she is ensconced in the "place prepared for her by God", where she does not have to struggle to get by but is "nourished" by God. This womanly, Marian Church cannot be affected by the power of the dragon: "The gates of hell shall not prevail against it." The rock of Peter is safeguarded there too, which is why he is told, "Put your sword into its sheath." Paul and John Paul II go through the world without any sword: it is enough for them to bear witness; that is their strongest weapon, and the successor of Peter can always find new strength, for this witness is a Marian Church.

2

GIVING BIRTH IN PAIN

GIVING BIRTH IN PAIN

Advent

Mary's nine-month Advent was not without pain. Even if she was preserved from original sin so as to be able to give the complete assent that was necessary for God's Word to become man, this does not mean that she was therefore spared the pains that from the very beginning have been imposed on woman in childbirth: "I will greatly multiply your pain in childbearing; in pain you shall bring forth children" (Gen 3:16). What Mary has to suffer is expiation for Eve and her descendants. She stands in solidarity with the mother of the race precisely because she is free of sin, and she stands even more closely in solidarity with her people Israel, which as a whole is continually experiencing the birth pangs of the Messiah. She belongs to the completion of the covenant with the people that represents mankind as a whole; and precisely because she always already belongs to the promised New Covenant (Jer 31:31), she is in the most profound way possible linked with God's original covenant, which Paul on a single occasion calls the "old covenant" (2 Cor 3:14).

One does not need to point out how embarrassing her increasingly obvious pregnancy would have been for her: but for "the handmaid of the Lord", this was the least of her worries. Would she, a weak girl, be equal to the immense promise that she would bring into the world the Son of the Most High, as the angel had called him? That was in some way also the worry of the most faithful in Israel: How should something so pure and indivisible as the Messiah of the final age be able to emerge from this continually sinful and divided people? Even if the imagination might think of him as existing beforehand hidden in heaven, Israel would nevertheless be concerned with his arrival on earth.

What Mary underwent during her Advent was above all mental and spiritual suffering: every pregnancy that is undergone in a genuinely human way involves a certain intercession, a certain suffering on behalf of the child, which is given to him at his birth as an invisible gift of grace to take on his journey through life. It is a selfless hope, a commending of the child to God or—if one does not know God—to the invisible powers that guide the fate of men and women. With what concern must Mary have prayed for the child growing within her and how she must have worried about him in advance! Did she have a premonition that the Messiah would have to suffer? We do not know. But some overpowering fate must await him. Simeon in the temple would confirm this to her: "Behold, this child is set for the fall and rising of many in Israel, and for a sign that is spoken against." For woman, pregnancy does not proceed without some element of fear; for Mary, it would not proceed without some presentiment of the Cross. From the outset she had a share in it that could not be defined.

We do not know to what extent physical hardships were linked with this mental and spiritual suffering; but it is quite possible that they lasted until shortly before the birth, which in the end took place as a miracle, as the sudden beginning of something final and definitive. At the birth every pain was dissolved in pure light: *Weih-Nacht*, holy night. How her womb opened and closed again we do not know, and it is pointless to speculate about an event that for God was child's play, something much less consequential than the original overshadowing by the Holy Spirit. Someone who accepts this first miracle as valid—as indeed a believer must, for otherwise Jesus would have had two fathers—should not lose any sleep over accepting the second miracle, the Virgin Birth. For Jews, the decisive use of the Greek word for "virgin" in the translation of the old Hebrew prophecy "Behold, a young woman shall conceive" is truly astonishing (in Isaiah 7:14, "young woman" could assuredly be intended to mean "virgin"). And for this reason alone, it is fitting, from the virginal son onward, for virginal fruitfulness to become a specific "vocation" for men and women in the Church (1 Cor 7).

*"My little children, with whom I am
again in travail"*

If in the Church a virginal life in emulation of not
only Jesus but also Mary becomes a gift of grace,
then without doubt, such a life is bound up with
the pains that go along with pregnancy. If this way
of life is to be fruitful in a new and heightened way,
it must be a matter of vocation and not merely of
bachelorhood or spinsterhood. It must involve a
conscious and free surrender of one's physical fertility, which, after all, can only bring forth that which
is doomed to die, in order to obtain a share in the
new fruitfulness of the Cross and Resurrection that
is able to generate and bear what is truly immortal.
It is in this that Christian virginity is distinguished
most profoundly from other religions' ascetic prac-
tices that are hostile to life: one can say that it is
their direct opposite. This is not only because of
its fruitfulness but also because it is an explicit gift
from God that people do not reach out and take for
themselves but that they receive as a grace. Paul may
have wished that all should live as he did, but since
celibacy is a matter not of one's own decision but of
a calling or vocation (*klēsis*), everyone should take
up the state of life he is given by God (1 Cor 7:24).

Paul, who could not yet know how Marian his
virginity was, was very conscious of living it as a
pregnancy linked with birth pangs for his "children".
He carried in his womb the Galatian community,

which was inclined to apostasy, and he was "again in travail until Christ be formed in you" (Gal 4:19). He consciously suffered less for communities that were not yet born than for those which had indeed been established but had not yet come to full term in the apostolic womb. "Who is made to fall, and I am not indignant?" (2 Cor 11:29). This pain is laid on him by God himself, and it is so intolerable that "three times I besought the Lord about this, that it should leave me".

But this was not to be: "My grace is sufficient for you, for my power is made perfect in weakness" (2 Cor 12:9). Once Paul had grasped this, then "I will all the more gladly boast of my weaknesses, that the power of Christ may rest upon me. For the sake of Christ, then, I am content with weaknesses, insults, hardships, persecutions, and calamities", for all this created room in him for Christ's effective action (2 Cor 12:9–18). He is hardly concerned if the community regards him as not very gifted, because this gives him the opportunity to take its failure upon himself and give it new birth as strength from his weakness. "So death is at work in us, but life in you" (2 Cor 4:12). And the death that is at work in him is no ordinary death, or even a purely ascetic one, but solely the fruitfully redemptive death of Jesus Christ, who himself gives him the power to beget for all time from himself those who believe and love. "For he was crucified in weakness, but lives by the power of God" (2 Cor 13:4).

Paul gives the most comprehensive description of this fruitfulness that comes from the abstemious life of Jesus, and through him, the life of his mother, of Joseph, of John the Baptist, of the beloved disciple, and of so many Christians who have followed after. One need only think of the power of spiritual fecundity that has been given to the great founders of religious orders like Benedict, Francis, or Ignatius Loyola: a power that has not been exhausted over hundreds and thousands of years. It is the decisive reason why the Catholic Church, and in its way the Orthodox as well, has insisted so obstinately on priestly celibacy. If celibacy is lived consciously and with a due willingness to "suffer the pangs of birth until Christ be formed" in those entrusted to the celibate's care, and if the Marian origin of this grace is understood, then it can often "be known" almost tangibly "by its fruits".

Giving Birth to Heaven

Mary as a virgin with her son gave birth to the last age, for she is the epitome and the embodiment of Israel, which awaited the birth pangs of the Messiah as a sign that the dawn of the final and definitive world had broken upon us. The Son, however, who comes from the Father and is going to the Father (Jn 16:28), has prepared the way to heaven for us: "I am the way; I go to prepare a place for you" (Jn 14:2, 6). The heaven he is preparing for us is not some ready-made place; one must rather say that it is through his going there, his ascension into heaven, that it first really comes into being for us. Being in heaven means being "at home with the Lord" (2 Cor 5:8). "My desire is to depart and be with Christ, for that is far better" (Phil 1:23). Inasmuch as we are with Christ, we will share in his being in his Father's house—and still less is the Father himself a "place". This sharing is precisely what awaits us in heaven. Of course the transfigured Son is not alone in his heaven, but the innumerable throng that is gathered around him only has access to this eternity through him, "the firstborn from the dead, that in everything he might be preeminent; for in him all the fullness of God was pleased to dwell" (Col 1:18–19). This fullness is also the fullness of heaven: the "heavenly Jerusalem" is not only forever his bride, but also the entire complement of his members, his fully grown body.

Christians may rightly talk about hoping to "get to heaven"; but at the same time, they know that there is such a thing as earning one's place in heaven—or, to put it another way, "laying up for oneself treasures in heaven" (Mt 6:20)—and in that way, by means of a truly Christian life making ready the place in heaven that has been set aside for them: indeed, one can truly speak of giving birth to one's heaven at the end of an earthly pregnancy. Of course, this is not accomplished by one's own power, but by the power of faith in Christ and our configuration to him. If we take this into consideration— and the idea is not presumptuous—then the proclamation of Mary's physical assumption into heaven will no longer seem so odd to us.

Our existence began on earth—we are initially all born into the community of sinners—and it is only through baptism or by some other means of grace that we are taken into the community of those blessed by God through Christ. Mary, on the other hand, has a place in God's plan of salvation that cannot be compared with ours: she is an indispensable component of the execution of this plan; her freedom from sin is the condition under which the Word of God is able to become flesh. This was not at first a physical affair, but required complete agreement, like a spiritual womb, so that God could insert himself into the human community. Mary's entire person, soul and body indivisibly united, was the vessel for his entry. From this insight that Mary in her entirety had her origin in God's heavenly plan, the Church understands also that Mary herself could only be taken up into this fully realized wholeness if she had a place there all along. Of course one can say that she too labored toward heaven through her earthly "service", all her sufferings up to the Pietà, but she was from the outset so free and so determined that there could be no accident, no miscarriage, in her earthly pregnancy that pointed to heaven.

We poor sinners pray to her about the hour of our death: she is the "gate of heaven"—much more so than Peter the gatekeeper—who makes it possible for us to reach her son: *per Mariam ad Iesum.* She is the help we need for our birth into heaven to be successful.

The Old Covenant knew nothing of heaven: the psalmist's lament that with death all praise of God comes to an end is an alarming enough indication of this. Even those who believed before Christ, who were on pilgrimage toward what was promised and saw the homeland from afar, "did not receive what was promised": "apart from us they should not be made perfect" (Heb 11:39–40). First the "first-born from the dead" had to be raised up (Col 1:18): "Christ the first fruits, then at his coming those who belong to Christ" (1 Cor 15:23), so that the seer of Revelation can be told: "Blessed are the dead who die in the Lord henceforth" (Rev 14:13). Henceforth heaven can be born from the pains of earth, and the more the history of this world follows Christ in the way of the Cross, the more fruitful this giving birth can become.

Is it not odd that the "new Jerusalem" is said to "come down out of heaven from God" (Rev 21:2), when what is meant is that the earthly Jerusalem, as symbol of God's city and kingdom on earth, must ultimately be raised up to heaven and transfigured? But "henceforth" there is no longer any earthly Jerusalem at all, since the earthly Christ has become a heavenly—yet always incarnate—Christ. Paul tells us this in a roundabout way: the present earthly Jerusalem "is in slavery with her children. But the Jerusalem above is free, and she is our mother. For it is written, 'Rejoice, O barren one that dost not bear; break forth and shout, thou who are not in travail; for the desolate hath more children than she who hath a husband' " (Gal 4:25–27, quoting Is 54:1). The "barren one" is the virginal one; it is she who has the many children. Whether we now call her Mary or the heavenly Church or "our Mother above", it is she through whom and because of whom we poor sinners can be fruitful.

3

MARY, THE MEMORY
OF THE CHURCH

MARY, THE MEMORY
OF THE CHURCH

Mary's Pondering

The description of Mary as the memory of the
Church comes from a homily that the Holy Father
Pope John Paul II preached in St. Peter's on Jan-
uary 1, 1987, the feast of Mary, Mother of God,
in which he announced his encyclical on Mary,
Redemptoris Mater. We need to think a bit about this
description. It may seem a little new and unfamiliar
to us, alongside the many titles that have already
been assigned to Mary, but it draws our attention to
a quite important aspect of her relationship to the
Church, to us.

Twice Luke emphasizes that, hearing what was
said about her child, "Mary kept all these things,
pondering them in her heart" (Lk 2:19): concerning
what the shepherds told her and what Jesus himself said when his parents "did not understand" his
explanation for staying behind in Jerusalem (Lk
2:51). It was precisely because these sayings were
so mysterious that Mary had reason to ponder them
continually. Indeed, already at the Annunciation,

when the angel told her that God had a very special
grace in mind for her, while she was afraid (as was
everyone in the Bible who was confronted by the
word of God), she "considered in her mind what
sort of greeting this might be" (Lk 1:29). She is
continually involved in mysteries whose meanings
tower above her, but instead of resigning herself to
bafflement, she makes room for them in her heart
in order to mull them over continually (the Greek
word Luke uses at 2:19, *symballein*, really means to
throw together, to compare, and hence to consider
from all possible angles).

This is to say that by no means does she understand everything completely from the first moment
onward; instead, she has to work tirelessly to understand all these overpowering ideas as well as she can.
She has one original experience on which to base
her understanding: she was told she would conceive
a son, not by a man but by the Holy Spirit. And
behold, she, the virgin, conceives. And this son was
described to her as the "Son of the Most High"
(Lk 1:32): How is a Jewish woman to grasp that
Yahweh has a son? But her pregnancy is a fact. The
Incarnation is a fact on which she is continually to
ponder without comprehending it.

And how did the incomprehensible come to
be? "The Holy Spirit will come upon you, and the
power of the Most High will overshadow you"
(Lk 1:35). The angel announced to her not just the
Incarnation but essentially the entire mystery of

the Trinity: "The Lord is with you"—that is Yah-weh, the Father-God, whom she knows. And then, as she ponders this: "You will conceive a son" who at the same time will be the son of David. When she asks about her own role in this, since this son cannot come from a man, he answers: "The Holy Spirit". The Trinity is therefore included in what befalls her. There is endless opportunity for pondering on the basis of that fact, which has such profundity and in which she saw the fulfillment of all God's prom-ises (the son of David is a reference to the Messiah) and probably also caught a glimpse of his Passion. And this pondering grew all the more intense as the child grew and left home, founded a new family (Mt 12:46–50), and was finally defeated, condemned, and crucified. Now she is needed once again: she must share in the experience of this fact and finally (in the darkness of noncomprehension) come to understand what Simeon had said: "A sword will pierce through your own soul also" (Lk 2:35). Let us not forget that from the start she possesses the full grace of the Holy Spirit, and that therefore this "pondering" over the facts she has experienced and lived through cannot be a matter of just stumbling around in the dark but is a quiet, silent growth in insight, and indeed in the insight of the simple "handmaid of the Lord".

She had already grasped everything at the wed-ding at Cana! She understood that she might plead for the poor who had nothing more to offer, because her son could fix things if he wanted to;

that she should not be discouraged by his refusal—
it is as if she had already understood the parables
of the person who knocked on his friend's door
at midnight (Lk 11:5–13) and of the unrighteous
judge (Lk 18:1–8); and that finally she should leave
everything to the son, the surest means of procur-
ing everything she prayed for according to God's
will: "Do whatever he tells you" (Jn 2:5). She had
already grasped much of dogma and of the Christian life in practice, simply on the basis of her original unconditional Yes. And we may boldly add
that under the Cross she also understood that one
must say Yes to what is most incomprehensible.
All this remains steadfastly in her memory. Nobody
else has such an uninterrupted memory from the
first moment of the Incarnation to the Cross, to the
Pietà, to the burial, and to the Resurrection. Here
we must quote Ignatius Loyola: Jesus appeared
first to "the Virgin Mary. Though this is not mentioned explicitly in the Scripture it must be considered as stated when Scripture says that He appeared
to many others. For Scripture supposes that we
have understanding, as it is written, 'Are you also
without understanding?' "[1]

And when Mary is then handed over to John
and thus to the apostles and to the Church as their
mother, we see her praying together with the

[1] Ignatius of Loyola, *Spiritual Exercises*, trans. Louis Puhl (Westmin-
ster, Md.: Newman Press, 1951), no. 299.

assembled Church for the Holy Spirit (Acts 1:14). Does Pentecost have a meaning for her too?

Mary and Pentecost

Here we should entrust ourselves to the wisdom of Romano Guardini:

> There must have been something divinely great when by the light of the Spirit everything became clear to her who "kept all these things in her heart": the context and interconnection of Jesus' existence were revealed. Throughout the years of Jesus' public life she had to maintain her confidence in heroic faith: now she received the answer, resplendent and solving everything.
>
> It is easy to think that she must always have understood the Lord, better than anyone else. Humanly speaking—to the extent that in this context one can talk of the human—without a doubt this was so. Historically no one else was able like her to provide information about him. But on the other side it is not without purpose that the Gospel says that she "did not understand the saying which he spoke to them". Probably she could just not have borne a real, complete understanding. The way of genuine experience of life lived in faith and love is greater than the anticipation of things which in God's guidance have their place only later. To recognize that the child, the boy, the youth, the man who lived in her company was the Son of

God in the sense that became manifest after Pentecost would probably have put her in an intolerable situation. That security without which existence as a mother is not possible would have disappeared. Now however God's mystery can be revealed, to the extent that this is possible on earth. She does not any longer need any protection against what is too great for human understanding. She is able to carry together in her mind the two statements, "He is the Son of the eternal Father" and "He is your son", without breaking down or merely becoming confused. Indeed, in this unity she recognizes the ineffable content of her vocation.[2]

Guardini's description of the effect of the Spirit on Mary at Pentecost—when, as innumerable medieval representations of the event portray, she becomes the center and focus of the Spirit-enlightened Church—is no blot on her perfection but rather allows us to see it as something genuinely human. What is unique about her is that the Spirit of Pentecost essentially does nothing other than present to her the content of her own experience as her memory had retained it: a memory that contains all the central dogmas of revelation in their complete unity and interwovenness.

We do not know if Mary received communion at a celebration of the Eucharist; but she knows better than any saint or sinner what it means to

[2] Die Mutter des Herrn (Würzburg: Werkbund-Verlag, 1956), 53–61.

accept the Son completely into oneself; she stands, as it were, behind every communion as the *ecclesia immaculata* that completes and perfects what we have done incompletely and imperfectly. Certainly she did not receive the sacrament of penance, but nobody else has laid his entire soul so bare before God, and this not just from time to time but at every moment of her existence. In this sense she is for the Church the "seat of wisdom", not because she knows more abstract truths than the most learned theologian but because she has most perfectly "heard the word of God and kept it" (Lk 11:28) and has been most completely and perfectly enlightened by the Holy Spirit about her acceptance of God's word. In Augustine's well-known phrase, she conceived the Son of the Father "first with her spirit and then with her body", and hence she also bore him "first with her spirit and then with her body" and gave him to the Church and to the world—not just at one single moment in history but at every moment of the history of the Church and of the world. In her it becomes apparent that the perfect faith which shared in making the Son's Incarnation possible contributes to perfect experience and perfect knowledge. Certainly she finally came to know the entire depth and breadth of her place in God's plan of salvation when she was assumed body and soul into heaven, and she kept this knowledge to be disseminated to the faithful.

The Teacher of the Church

Mary's wish for us throughout the ages of the Church is not that we should venerate her as an individual but that we should recognize the depth of God's love in the work of his Incarnation and redemption. Since she lived in the house of the beloved disciple, it would be astonishing if her presence and words were not a part of the inspiration for the Gospel of the love of the triune God made manifest in Christ. Certainly it is telling that the first apparition of our Lady we hear about from trustworthy sources is the vision of Origen's pupil Gregory the Wonderworker, recounted by Gregory of Nyssa, that he had while preparing to be ordained as a bishop. While he was pondering the Scriptures, a figure appeared to him, an old man in the attitude and dress of a priest, who told him he would show him divine wisdom in order to remove his uncertainty. Then he gestured sideways with his hand and showed him another figure of superhuman dignity and almost unbearable splendor. This figure told the first figure, John the Evangelist, that he should expound the mystery of faith to the young man, whereupon John said he would gladly comply with the wishes of the Mother of the Lord and explained the mystery of the Trinity to Gregory in clear words. Gregory wrote down at once what was said and later preached about it to the people (*Patrologia graeca* vol. 10, cols. 984–88, vol. 46, cols. 909–13). It is one of the finest and clearest credal formulas that we have.

Mary's wishes are also made clear in the words that Ephraem the Syrian put in her mouth as an address to her son: "While I gaze on your outward form which can be seen with physical eyes, my spirit comprehends your hidden form. With my eyes I see the form of Adam, in your hidden form I see the Father dwelling in you. It is only to me that you have shown your glory in both forms. May the Church too, like your mother, see you both in your visible and in your mysterious form!"

It is only in heaven that we shall appreciate how much of the Church's understanding of the faith she owes to Mary, and indeed the "simple" understanding much more than the "clever and wise". It would thus be impossible to write a history of Mary's teaching through the centuries. But we can venture to say something about the sense and meaning of the apparitions of our Lady, which have been so numerous in recent times. Because Mary was so contemplative on earth, says Adrienne von Speyr, she can be so active in heaven, specifically by letting the Church share in the superabundance of her memory. Simply by the act of showing herself, she already leads us into the mystery of what the Church is in her essential nature: a pure work of God's grace. Mary is able, precisely in a spirit of complete humility, to point to herself because she is thereby pointing to nothing other than what

God's almighty grace is capable of and at the same time what we should strive for in order to become proper vessels for this grace, in order to play the key role of the Church (as the body and bride of Christ) correctly in her mission of salvation for the world.

Again and again the Rosary has played a role in recent Marian apparitions: Mary has fingered the beads along with those praying the Rosary. Why should this be? So that we should prefer praying to her over praying to Christ or the Father? On the contrary, it is so that we should look at the mysteries of Jesus' life—and thereby at the mysteries of the trinitarian drama of salvation—from her point of view, according to her memory. Our eyes are bleary and dull: if you will forgive the metaphor, we must put on Mary's spectacles in order to see accurately. "He who was scourged for our sake": what this means only becomes somewhat clear to us if we are aware of the effect this scourging had on Mary's mind and heart. The point is not just to generate a little sympathy: the weeping daughters of Jerusalem were turned back on the way to the Cross. But his mother walked alongside, unrecognized and veiled, in complete strength and at the same time weakness: her heart is the true veil of the legendary Veronica. What Christ is for her, what God is for her, becomes the primal and primary image of what he should be for us, and this is accomplished when in simplicity we try to see the mysteries of our redemption through her eyes.

We are forgetful. Things we have already heard too often fade in our memory. But Mary's memory is, after thousands of years, as fresh as it was on the first day. Let us allow her to appear daily before our eyes, as she may appear visibly to children she has chosen. There is no chasm between them and us. Rather, it is as John the Evangelist says, that for living Christians, faith and knowledge are one. "We have believed, and have come to know, that you are the Holy One of God" (Jn 6:69). "Now we know that you know all things ...; by this we believe that you came from God" (Jn 16:30). Faith is the surrender of the entire person: because Mary surrendered everything from the start, her memory was the unsullied tablet on which the Father, through the Spirit, could write his entire Word.

4

MARRIAGE AND VIRGINITY

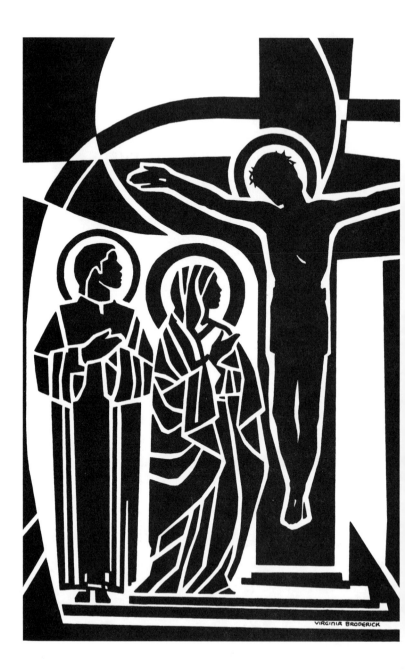

VIRGINIA BRODERICK

MARRIAGE AND VIRGINITY

The Heritage of Israel

Mary is unique, but that does not mean she is isolated, and Marian piety should not isolate her either. Many portrayals show her as part of a community: pictures of her with St. Anne show her in the succession of generations to which she belongs; the meeting with St. Elizabeth wonderfully symbolizes the profound inner unity between the Old and New Covenants; Mary's child blesses his precursor, John the Baptist, while often one sees the two children playing together watched over by their mothers; Mary's exchange of rings with Joseph is portrayed, but even more often, her standing with John at the foot of the Cross; finally there is the apostles' astonishment at seeing her taken up into heaven away from a flowery tomb. However lonely she may have been, she was never isolated. When she encountered the angel, she was already definitively engaged, and from the Cross her son placed her equally firmly in the middle of the Church.

In her, the prefigurements in Israel were fulfilled and more than fulfilled. Here two things must be mentioned: the sanctity of marriage in ancient Israel and the ways in which the prophets portrayed God's position as Israel's husband.

Because Israel was awaiting its future Messiah, it held marriage sacred. Barrenness was considered shameful because it meant no contribution was being made to the coming of the Messiah (Gen 30:23, 1 Sam 1:5–8). When Elizabeth, who was "barren" and "advanced in years", conceived, she said: "Thus the Lord has done to me in the days when he looked upon me, to take away my reproach among men" (Lk 1:25). What is even more significant is that God himself comes to help the human lack of fertility: when Abraham was helped to beget Isaac, the son of the promise, when Zechariah was helped to beget John the Baptist, the question can always be asked whether it was God or man who really did the begetting. As far as what happened to Abraham is concerned, the fact that his body, "as good as dead", bore fruit counted as a resurrection from the dead for him (Rom 4:17–19, Heb 11:19): he knew that God was acting through him. Because Zechariah did not have this pure faith, he was punished even though he begot the child. What man cannot do, God can do in him, and man must recognize this. This line culminates in Joseph, whom we shall discuss in what follows.

First, however, we must look at the second theme in Israel that points to the future. The people's adultery in their covenant with God must be brought

before their eyes by gestures of the prophets: what
the prophets do and suffer to accomplish this is like
an incipient incarnation of the Divine Word. Jer-
emiah is forbidden, among many other things, to
marry: "You shall not take a wife, nor shall you
have sons or daughters in this place" (Jer 16:2), for
the prophet must make visible God's unwillingness
to have anything more to do with his unfaithful
spouse. Ezekiel is warned of the sudden death of his
wife, "the delight of your eyes", but told: "Yet you
shall not mourn or weep nor shall your tears run
down. Sigh, but not aloud; make no mourning for
the dead" (Ezek 24:15–17). Why? Because Yahweh
mourns no longer over the downfall and banish-
ment of his faithless people.

The most bitter of these tasks is the one laid upon
Hosea to marry a prostitute (Gomer was either a
prostitute from the start or else she was unfaithful
to the prophet) and to "have children of harlotry"
with her, in that the mother's guilt is transmitted to
the children. They are given suitable names, such
as "Not Pitied" (Hos 1:2–9). God explains that this
describes his relationship with his people, but he
finally opens up the prospect of a future reconcil-
iation with those who have been unfaithful (Hos
2:4–23). Here celibacy is not a punishment for the
prophets, who all obey, but a stern warning to the
disobedient. The theme that points to the future is
to be found in the prophets' complete obedience in
their use and nonuse of sexuality.

Mary and Joseph

Now perhaps we can understand better the kind of theological significance the marriage between Mary and Joseph has. This marriage is necessary not only so that Mary's child can count as a descendant of David but also in order to lead to the fulfillment of the religious sense of Old Testament marriage. Joseph thus accomplishes the two purposes mentioned above but does so while crossing the threshold of the final and definitive covenant. He brings to completion the fecundity of Abraham, who gave to God all the glory and understood his fruitfulness as a "resurrection from the dead" and thus allowed God to take over completely. For a husband whose life was centered on his marriage, this meant a renunciation on the basis of faith and at the same time a sharing in the virginal fruitfulness of his wife. Here Joseph is completely within the domain of the New Covenant: physically, it might seem that he is merely the child's foster-father, but spiritually, he has a very much more profound share in God's fatherliness by assenting silently to the renunciation demanded by the angel. His hidden virginal fruitfulness should not be forgotten when Mary's grace is seen in its full light. The marriage that linked Joseph to Mary is a model both for married people and for celibates in Christ's Church. Admittedly this marriage points predominantly backward; it is the completion of marriage as well as of prophetic obedience in Israel. It hardly points forward to the questionable ideal of "Josephite marriages". What points forward is the link between Mary and John.

Mary and John

The last thing that Jesus established as he was dying on the Cross, before everything was fulfilled according to the Scriptures—that is, the community of Mary and John as a community of mother and son—no longer has anything in common with marriage. Here, human fruitfulness has finally transcended the sphere of sexuality, but not in the direction of hostility toward the body and "spiritualization" of it, but in the direction of a Church whose core is formed by the eucharistic link between Christ and his "bride" and "wife" (Rev 21:9). Mary, the virgin who gives birth, is the *Realsymbol*—both a representation and a living presentation—of this bride, her unassailable origin, and her final goal (everything that will belong to the Church finds its place between this beginning and this end), and John is the Realsymbol of the son of this Church, the only person who was explicitly "loved" by Christ. In this way Saint Ephraem can say that each of these two figures sees Christ in the other: in Mary, John sees the perfect origin of his beloved master; in John, Mary sees the embodiment of him whom her son had loved and still loves and who did his best to reciprocate this love.

From this original cell of the Church established at the Cross comes everything that will develop into the organism of the Church: Peter, already designated as the rock, who has denied Christ, is endowed with Johannine love so as to be able to withstand the Lord's question: "Do you love me more than these?" and thereupon to be granted the promise of crucifixion. John, who has Jesus' mother with him, is a member of the college of apostles, and one so distinguished that at the beginning of the Acts of the Apostles he always appears along with Peter: he thus becomes a link between the spotlessly holy Church and the hierarchically organized Church. Both are indivisibly one, both are visible in their unity and invisible in the divine mystery: to separate them from each other would be fatal for the Church and would be to deny the bond between Mary and John established at the Cross.

It is eminently appropriate if the fatherly head of the Church ("pope" means father) continually turns anew to the Mother of the Church to ask for support and fruitfulness for the work of his ministry. John, who linked Mary with Peter, can move into the background (by no means does he make a superior center): it is enough if he has the promise from the Lord that he will "remain", and indeed, it was not as if Peter were in charge of supervising the sphere of love: "If it is my will that he remain until I come, what is that to you?" (Jn 21:22–23).

To conclude our consideration of the relationship between Mary and Joseph and that between Mary and John, we can take a look at Christian marriage. According to Paul, inasmuch as marriage is a sacrament, it is the reflection of the relationship between Christ and his Church. Here the apostle looks back to Genesis, where Eve is formed out of the side of Adam, for certainly the Church has been formed out of the eucharistic body of Christ and has thus become simultaneously his body and his bride. The husband must therefore directly imitate the model of Christ: "Husbands, love your wives, as Christ loved the church and gave himself up for her" (Eph 5:25). He is to love her as one loves one's own flesh and cherishes it, "as Christ does the Church, because we are members of his body" (vv. 29–30).

With regard to the Church, one cannot say that she sacrifices herself for Christ, as if to make him "holy and without blemish" (v. 27). Her love for him has another form: respect or reverent awe (v. 33). "As the Church is subject to Christ, so let wives also be subject in everything to their husbands" (v. 24). What becomes of the equality of the sexes here? It remains where it says: "Be subject to one another out of reverence for Christ" (v. 21) or: "For as woman was made from man, so man is now born of woman" (1 Cor 11:12). In this statement the position of Mary—never prominent in Paul—is once again clear.

If the Church, eucharistically considered, comes from Christ, so Christ, physically considered, comes

from Mary. And with the child and even with the
grown-up Jesus there would have been something
like respect or rather reverent awe for Mary's maternal authority, since it was to her that he owed his
being, and he praised her for hearing and keeping
the word of God (Lk 11:28). But this mutual respect
in love does not stop Mary, in view of the dignity of her child, from complying with his wishes
when she does not understand them. And here she
fits into the Pauline picture of how a wife should
behave toward her husband. We should not speak
too easily of this view being sociologically outdated.
Mary is not a feminist: she remains the "handmaid
of the Lord", even when she can become the "all-
powerful intercessor" with her son.

5

THE POOR

THE POOR

Magnificat

We know nothing about Mary's financial circumstances, nor do they play any part in her song of rejoicing. And that is what the Magnificat really is: she is not surprised that God "has regarded the low estate of his handmaiden" but simply rejoices in the fact, since in this gesture she recognizes the God of Israel who has always acted thus.

The song that Luke puts in her mouth is primarily modeled on the song of Hannah (1 Sam 2:1–10), which speaks of practically nothing other than this inversion of earthly circumstances in which one recognizes the action that characterizes God. Where Mary sings: "He has put down the mighty from their thrones, and exalted those of low degree; he has filled the hungry with good things, and the rich he has sent empty away" (Lk 1:52–53), Hannah sang: "Those who were full have hired themselves out for bread, but those who were hungry have ceased to hunger. . . . He raises up the poor from the dust; he lifts the needy from the ash heap, to make them sit with princes and inherit a seat of honor" (1 Sam

2:5, 8). In her assertions, which are echoed in many other Old Testament passages, Hannah goes still further when she says: "The Lord kills and brings to life; he brings down to Sheol and raises up. The Lord makes poor and makes rich; he brings low, he also exalts" (vv. 6–7). This can make good sense in the context of the New Testament as well if one considers that God loves the poor and lowly, while "the haughty he knows from afar" (Ps 138:6), and that he had his Son descend to the realm of the dead in order from there to exalt him over all things.

It is not his justice but explicitly his mercy that Mary praises in all the reversals and inversions that God has brought about: "His mercy is on those who fear him from generation to generation", and throughout its whole history he has adopted "his servant Israel, in remembrance of his mercy" (Lk 1:50, 54). If as the result of being singled out, the servant of God had puffed itself up to become one of the mighty, God's mercy could not have been demonstrated in its case. It is only for the "low estate of his handmaiden" that "he who is mighty has done great things ..., and holy is his name" (vv. 48–49). The poor man lying in the dust of the ash heap has no particular quality in himself that would make God raise him up: the mercy shown to him has its ground only in God himself, whose free grace finds a welcome in the emptiness of poverty while it seems it would not be needed in the overcrowded space of the rich, the high and the mighty.

In the case of Hannah—and in the whole of the Old Testament—the starting-point for the elevating and liberating effect of God's grace is first of all material, social poverty (and here, the rich and the powerful are also labeled the oppressors and the "enemies" of God, which is not the case in Mary's song) in order to emphasize all the more the sheer dependence on God that is engendered by the powerlessness of the poor: in the case of Mary, this takes center stage.

The "low estate of his handmaiden" that God regards is the chosen place for all divinely brought about reversals in the world, the core of the divine revolution of love and its daily work of liberation. Mary is the personification of true liberation theology when she exuberantly brings to perfection the deep insight of the Old Testament, an insight made more profound in her.

"Do whatever he tells you"

Mary plays a mysterious role at the wedding at Cana. The couple whose wedding it was were clearly friends of the family in Nazareth: the mother was invited (her husband was presumably no longer alive) as well as her son along with his friends, who were probably regarded as his first followers. Mary is one among many other guests. But she is the first to notice the embarrassing situation these probably

not very well-off people are in, and if she draws
her son's attention to it, it is certainly not because
she expects him to work a miracle (hitherto he had
not worked any—Jn 2:11) but in the hope that he
would find a solution. What is to be noted here is
Mary's awareness of the needs of the poor and her
instinctive sense that her son must be told about it
and that he will somehow be able to provide help.

And then it is as if the whole scene has moved
up to a higher plane. Jesus has begun his ministry:
he is no longer this person's son. And in his ministry he no longer sees Mary as his own mother but
as "the woman", the other, the "helpmate", who,
however, will only take on her own proper role
when he finally, on the Cross, becomes the "new
Adam". She has already suffered: the sword has
already pierced her soul. He, on the other hand, is
only now marching toward his "hour". Then, in
complete poverty and stripped of everything, even
of God, he will change the wine into his blood: the
effusive response to every most audacious entreaty.
The "woman" whom he tries to put off—"What
have you to do with me?"—is, however, already
from the start the Church, and as such she has a
right to insist on her "request" (actually, just her
pointing out of the people's need). But she does
it in the most wonderful way that expresses everything at the same time: her complete disinterest and
surrender to his will, but also her confident hope;
and it is precisely by not pushing, by her lack of self-
will, that she prevails and the hour of the Cross is

anticipated: not yet is wine transformed into blood, but water into wine: "Do whatever he tells you." Perhaps nowhere is Mary's whole disposition more present than in this saying.

"And his mother and his brethren came"

In Cana we saw Mary with those who were materially poor. Here (Mk 3:31) we see her with those who are spiritually poor. These "brethren"—cousins and other close relatives, described even today by Arabs as "brothers"—are annoyed by Jesus' extravagant behavior and think he is out of his mind. When he appears in Nazareth, they will take offense at his making himself out to be more important than his relatives: "Are not his sisters here with us?" (Mk 6:3). We have already seen that these people who did not believe in him urged him to go and take his act to Jerusalem instead: "For no man works in secret if he seeks to be known openly. If you do these things, show yourself to the world" (Jn 7:4).

One must imagine Mary among these people. She does not think of contradicting them or of setting herself apart from them as someone who knows better about everything. She listens to this kind of talk every day, possibly also to the reproach that she should have brought him up better and should not have put such ideas in his head. She belongs to the family. The immaculate belongs to the clan of sinners, the seat of wisdom belongs to the bottomless stupidity of humanity. One must listen to this clique of relatives discussing among themselves how they can put an end to this nonsense. Finally, they decide to send out an expedition so that they can see things for themselves, and his mother is dragged along. But they are sent packing, even when Jesus is told his mother is there. The family no longer counts for anything. It is a quite different family that matters now: those who believe and who do the will of God.

One can imagine what this company had to say to each other on the way home. Even though Mark puts the event earlier (3:21), it is quite probably at this point that the family came to the decision that he ought to be stopped for his own good. And it was not just a matter of words—words turned into actions: "His friends ... went out to seize him, for they said, 'he is beside himself.'" Mary was living in their midst. At what point James, one of Jesus' brothers, came to believe in him we do not know: he became Peter's deputy in Jerusalem when the latter had to flee from the city after being freed from prison.

Mary does not stand out from the group. She remains so inconspicuous that the synoptic Gospels do not even notice her among the devout women at the foot of the Cross. Several of them are named, but she is not. Perhaps she stands there, together with John, keeping to herself, distant from the others, lost in the crowd of Roman soldiers and of people who had come to gape and mock and the crowds streaming in and out of the city past the crosses on the day before the feast: some poor woman.

6

THE WOUND CREATES SPACE

VIRGINIA BRODERICK

THE WOUND CREATES SPACE

Humility Is Unconscious

When the girl is greeted as "full of grace" by the angel, she is afraid, for the phrase sheds light on her own essential nature, which she had never reflected on. "Poverty of spirit" (or, in other words, humility) is not some ascertainable virtue—like capability, suitability, or competence, which one can be conscious of—but the unconsidered awareness that everything that one is and has is a loan and gift from God and is only there to bring the giver into the spotlight. It is typical that in its psalms Israel has no word for "thank" and instead talks of "praise" (before the entire community). It is only the Pharisee in the temple who says (in Greek): "God, I thank thee that I am not like other men" (Lk 18:11). He is giving thanks for something he has identified in himself; the psalms, by contrast, only praise God the giver. When the woman in the crowd praises as blessed "the breasts that you sucked", Jesus shifts the focus away from what Mary has, and can thus offer, to what one receives and may only keep as a gift: "Blessed rather are those who hear the word of God and keep it" (Lk 11:27–28). He focuses on those who are so inwardly impoverished and emptied out that they have divested themselves of their inmost core, their "conscience", in order to yield the place to the word of God.

It is only the sinner who twists himself back onto his ego: the person who is sinless (the only one there is) does not know this backward glance but looks steadfastly forward to what is good, and "no one is good but God alone" (Mk 10:18). It is precisely this lack of knowledge about her own sinlessness that makes Mary the "seat of wisdom". Wisdom is not something one possesses, but a radiant light from God, and "is easily discerned by those who love her, and is found by those who seek her" (Wis 6:12). Its light is given to the poor and humble especially, but always in such a way that they do not experience the light that now shines within and from them as their own; rather, they are always aware of where it comes from and of the movement of grace that bestows this light on them. Mary can only point to Jesus, just as Jesus can only point to the Father: "My teaching is not mine, but his who sent me" (Jn 7:16).

Wound as Refuge

Understood in the context of the beatitudes, "poverty" is painful deprivation; it goes hand in hand with hunger, tears, and persecution. On the basis of the Old Testament, this is obvious. But in the New Testament, the void of poverty becomes a gaping wound that at the same time creates space. The inmost sanctuary is pierced, and all that is hidden there streams out; blood and water. This happens to the dead body of Jesus, while the "sword [that] will pierce through your own soul" is driven into the living body of his mother and lays bare her beating heart: both hearts become places of refuge where sinners can hide in the same way as in the Middle Ages criminals on the run could find sanctuary at the altars of certain churches. "*In tua vulnera absconde me:* in the hollows of your wounds hide me from the police and their henchmen."

Such places of refuge come about through bleeding, and if a Longinus can put his lance to that use, the real weapon is "the word of God, sharper than any two-edged sword" and piercing deeper than any human scalpel can "to the division of soul and spirit" (Heb 4:12). In the Crucified One the soul that dies is divided from the spirit of mission that is breathed out with bowed head and given up to the Father and to the Church: in the mother who shares his suffering, whose "soul magnifies the Lord" and whose "spirit rejoices in God my Savior" (Lk 1:46–47), the sword pierces between praise and rejoicing: the rejoicing is borne away with the spirit to God, while the soul remains behind and, when the body is taken down from the Cross, can only sigh out the assent of praise in the most profound darkness, in the utmost weakness.

It is here and nowhere else that sinners—whether oppressors or the weeping oppressed—can find refuge. As Claudel has written:

> Il n'y a pas d'ami sûr pour un pauvre, s'il ne trouve un plus pauvre que lui. C'est pourquoi viens, ma soeur accablée, et regarde Marie....
>
> Regarde Celle qui est là, sans plainte comme sans espérance, comme un pauvre qui trouve un plus pauvre, et tous deux se regardent en silence.[1]

It is the greater suffering that hides and thereby consoles: not with soothing words, not with promises that things will get better, but simply because the more profound pain as such goes on giving praise and only now does so adequately, just as from a broken jar of ointment comes a stronger aroma.

It remains an impenetrable mystery how this one mother's unfathomable yet temporal distress is transformed into the eternal praise of her transfiguration. Her heart remains as open as that of her son, who is continually offering his heart's blood in the eucharistic meal: "My blood is drink indeed, and

---

[1] "For the poor man there is no firm friend unless he finds someone poorer than himself. So come, my oppressed sister, and behold Mary.... Behold her who is there, without complaint as without hope, like a poor man who has found someone poorer, and both contemplate each other in silence." Paul Claudel, *Oeuvres poétiques* [Paris, 1962], 414.

he who does not drink it has no life in him." One should not place the mother's heart pierced by the sword far from the heart of her son, the heart that offers itself to all the poor as one yet poorer, even if its openness is only to be understood as pointing to the eternal openness of his heart to the Father. "I am the door", he says; she only says: "I am the handmaid, do whatever he tells you."

Her Protective Mantle

No one, whether he wants to or not, fails to find room under her mantle. For if her son has by his suffering chosen all people to be his brothers and sisters, she can be nothing other than their mother. And since she was his physical and spiritual mother to begin with and he never outgrows being her son, when she puts in a word with him for her children, it cannot be in vain. He is without doubt the just judge of us all, since the Father has given over to him all judgment (Jn 5:27) and power over all flesh (Jn 17:2); but God has not taken away from him who became man his mother and her maternal authority of intercession. Could the omnipotent intercession that is ascribed to her be simply pious exaggeration? At Cana she showed how she carries out her wishes despite all misgivings. There she was initially brushed off, and that rather abruptly: her son is thinking of his own duties, and Mary's request seems at the moment to run contrary to these. But what does the seat of wisdom do, the valiant woman in whom "the heart of her husband trusts" (Prov 31:11)? She simply appeals to that which is deepest in Jesus' own heart and mission, when she tells the servants: "Do whatever he tells you." Simplicity and artifice coincide when she penetrates through the level of justice in God to the more profound level of mercy. As a mother she can do this, because no proper mother punishes her children except out of love, and she is convinced that in this she is behaving correctly in a more profound way than whatever might be dictated by the abstract justice worked out by men for their state. As a woman, she has her heart where it ought to be and not in the brain; and she knows that a God who thought woman up and created her can also have his heart in no other place.

Does this not mean that Mary's role exceeds the bounds of propriety? She is after all merely the poor handmaid who has been banished to the wilderness of world history, spewed upon by the dragon, waiting out the endless one thousand two hundred sixty days. True, but in her birth pangs she is also the woman clothed with the sun, with the moon under her feet, and crowned with the twelve stars of the Lamb, the insignia of her incomparable motherhood. What she has borne is snatched away from her—it comes from God and belongs to God— while she remains behind in the wilderness. But she remains what she was and will be for all eternity, the mother. And what child, even if it were God, would forget the part played by his mother and his position with regard to her? "Honor your father and your mother ...": how should the Son of Man, who honored his heavenly Father in everything, not honor his earthly mother as well?

"With all your heart honor your father, and do not forget the birth pangs of your mother. Remember that through your parents you were born; and what can you give back to them that equals their gift to you?" (Sir 7:27–28).

INDEX